THE FASHION BOOK

CONTENTS

This item has to be renewed or returned on or before
the last date below

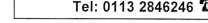

TWO WEEK LOAN

1 2 DEC 2016

THE
FS
BO

Buster Books

Written by Marie Vendittelli
Illustrated by Sophie Griotto

Translated by Annie Barton
Edited by Jen Wainwright
Concept and design by Laëtitia Robaeys
Cover design by Barbara Ward

Originally published in 2012 under the title 'Cahier de Styliste: Cultive ton look' by Editions de la Martinière, an imprint of La Martinière Groupe, Paris, France

First published in Great Britain in 2013 by Buster Books,
an imprint of Michael O'Mara Books Limited,
9 Lion Yard, Tremadoc Road, London SW4 7NQ

www.busterbooks.co.uk

A CIP catalogue record for this book is available from the British Library.

ISBN: 978-1-78055-113-5

10 9 8 7 6 5 4 3 2 1

This book was printed in February 2013 by
Tien Wah Press Ltd, 4 Pandan Crescent, Singapore, 128 475.

Are you ready to take your first steps in fashion?

Becoming a designer couldn't be easier. This book will show you how, with simple tricks, tips and techniques to tackle.

To start your journey into this fascinating world, it's useful to get a good grasp of fashion knowledge, and learn how the big names in style carved their own paths to success. You'll need to eat, sleep and breathe colours and fabrics so that you can create your own collections.

It's also time to start learning how to unleash your inner artist! Don't worry, even some of the world's best designers don't have super drawing skills. All you need are a few basic techniques to sketch a simple model silhouette that will show off your creations beautifully.

This book has one goal: to help you get started on your path to style stardom.

All the big designers were just like you when they started. So what are you waiting for?

express yourself!

HOW TO DRAW a SILHOUETTE

You don't need to have ten years of experience to have a go at designing cool clothes. Every designer has had to start at the beginning, by learning how to draw silhouettes (sometimes called outline models). Having these basic drawing skills under your belt will help you later on when you bring your designs to life.

TOP TIP

On a piece of paper – or in your very own designer's sketchbook (see page 104) – have a go at copying the mannequins you see in shop windows, using a few bold pencil strokes. Narrow waists, statement shoulder pads, A-line or pencil skirts ... you will already be familiar with the sorts of shapes you might come across. Trying these shapes out is the first step on the way to being able to draw lifelike models, full of movement.

Proportions of the body

For your drawings to be realistic, your models need to have the right proportions. There's a very simple technique to learn. All you need to do is split up the body into eight bits, each one the same height as the head you've drawn. These eight bits are listed below to help you.

1. Chin
2. Bust
3. Waist, elbows
4. Hips, wrists

5. Fingertips, thighs
6. Knees
7. Calves
8. Heels

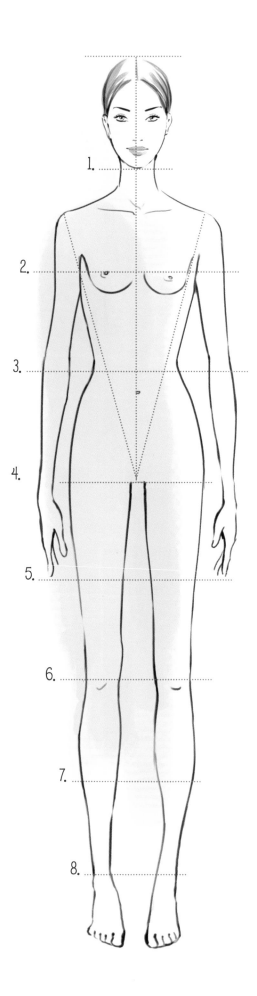

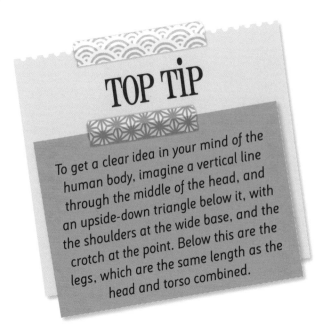

TOP TIP

To get a clear idea in your mind of the human body, imagine a vertical line through the middle of the head, and an upside-down triangle below it, with the shoulders at the wide base, and the crotch at the point. Below this are the legs, which are the same length as the head and torso combined.

Use this example to help you
DRAW YOUR FIRST SILHOUETTE.

Poses

To find out how an outfit will look, you need to make sure that the model you draw isn't as lifeless as a coat hanger! Try copying these drawings, which show basic model poses. Your silhouettes will soon look like a real designer's.

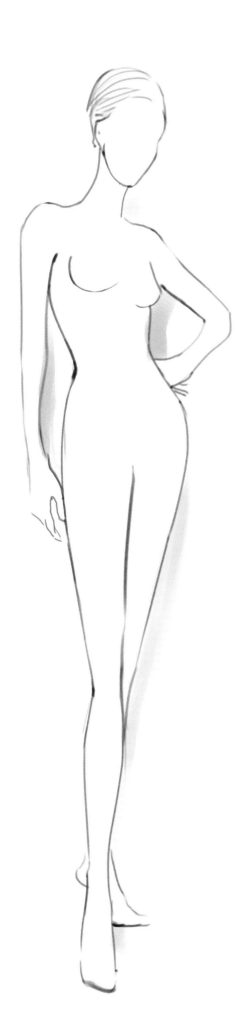

TOP TİP

Don't be afraid to exaggerate the poses you draw, adding swinging hips, sloping shoulders or curves. This will breathe more life into your drawings.

Classical painters were experts at drawing realistic figures.

Photocopy some pictures, especially by the great artists of the Italian Renaissance and the 19th century, then try to copy the outlines of their figures using just a few pencil strokes.

Here's one very simple trick for reproducing realistic poses: before you draw your silhouette, try to imagine how your skeleton is positioned when you're in that posture.

DRAWING THE HEAD

Most of your silhouette's personality will come from its face. Follow this example to draw the eyes, nose and mouth. Add some colour to your model by giving her some make-up.

FIVE HANDY HINTS
WHEN DRAWING HEADS:

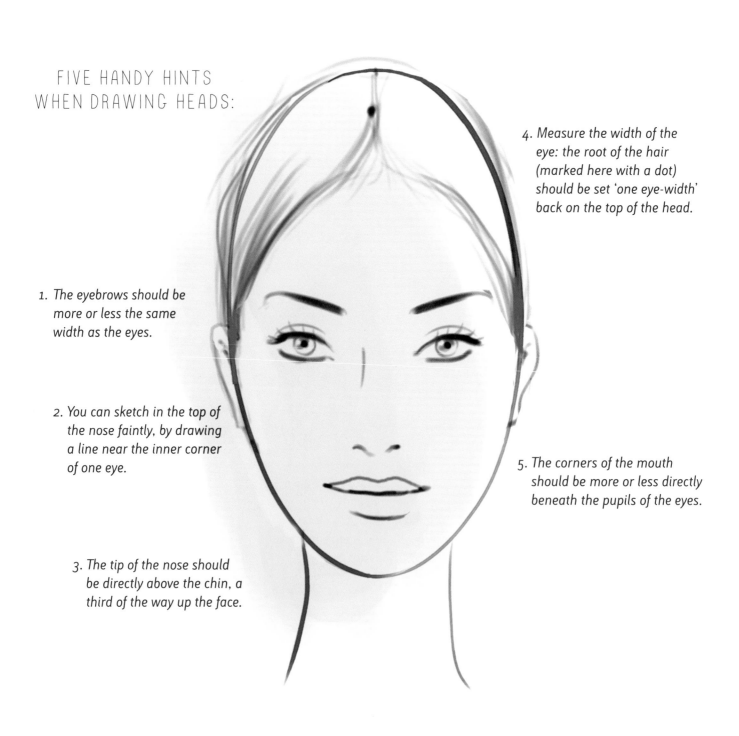

4. Measure the width of the eye: the root of the hair (marked here with a dot) should be set 'one eye-width' back on the top of the head.

1. The eyebrows should be more or less the same width as the eyes.

2. You can sketch in the top of the nose faintly, by drawing a line near the inner corner of one eye.

5. The corners of the mouth should be more or less directly beneath the pupils of the eyes.

3. The tip of the nose should be directly above the chin, a third of the way up the face.

COPY THE EXAMPLE OPPOSITE,
following the five handy hints.

TOP TIP

You can draw the outline for your figures in felt-tip, but the face will be softer if you use coloured pencils and focus on the details. Little by little, you will develop your own style and you'll see which techniques suit you best. You could also try using real blusher or eyeshadow on your paper – realistic glow guaranteed!

HOW TO DESIGN CLOTHES

People often wonder where designers get their ideas, and there isn't a simple answer. Some designers love looking at people in the streets and taking inspiration from them. Others don't focus at all on whether their clothing will be comfortable or easy to wear, they only concentrate on the 'look' they are creating. No matter where the ideas come from, designers are able to gather enough inspiration to create new trends.

To keep up with these trends and make them accessible to more people, large chain stores often produce variations of designers' styles. This might not seem very fair on the designers who came up with the original ideas, but it's certainly practical for shoppers who want to stay on-trend without breaking the bank.

DID YOU KNOW?

The trick of the big clothing chains is that they make you want to go shopping. To achieve this, they produce several new collections every year. To keep things fresh and exciting, the stock is changed roughly every six weeks. Another savvy shop trick is to regularly move the racks of clothes to different places in the shop, so you feel like things are different – and it works!

CHOOSING YOUR COLOURS

Studies have shown that people choose clothes first and foremost because of their colour. Amazingly, your eyes can see over 350,000 different colours, but you only need to know the basics in order to understand how to mix and match colours successfully.

There are two main families of colours: warm and cool.

The coldest of the cool colours is blue. Blue-greens, purples and greys containing a lot of blue are also cool colours.

In warm colours the hottest of the hot is red, complemented by a wide range of oranges, pinks, browns and yellows.

COLOUR CHART

TOP TIP

To understand how colours work, get three tubes of primary colour paint (red, blue and yellow), and a tube of black. On a piece of white paper, mix the colours in various ways and see what comes out. Choose the colours that you like the best and cut them out to use in your own colour chart.

COOL COLOURS

WARM COLOURS

CREATE YOUR OWN COLOUR PALETTE.
Use these pages to stick in samples of your favourite colours.

TOP TIP

*Observe, then go for it!
Shop windows of big department stores are designed by professionals. Study them closely. You'll see colour combinations there that you wouldn't expect, but that seem unbelievably obvious and attractive.*

To build up your own colour palette, lay out some fabric samples and try arranging them in different ways. It's often by using trial and error that you'll stumble upon the best colour mixes.

Mix and match them to make fun, unusual or simply pretty combinations.

DID YOU KNOW?

There's no such thing as a 'good' or 'bad' colour scheme. Your choice of colours just needs to suit the style of your collection. For example, choose plenty of bright colours for a youthful, vibrant look, or, for a simple, sophisticated and structured piece, go for darker shades and block colours.

colour Basics

NEUTRaLS

These belong to the warm colour group. Neutrals are perfect for basic wardrobe staples, and never go out of style. Best suited for colder weather.

BROWNS

Also quite neutral, browns can stay classic when paired with greys, or can be warmed up with oranges. A good colour for winter.

ORaNGES

These will pep up any piece of clothing, but it's best to reserve them for little touches here and there, to avoid the Halloween-pumpkin look.

YELLOWS

Even though they're beautifully bold, yellows are often overlooked because they don't suit everyone, and they're not always considered to be very chic.

GREENS

There are dozens of different greens to play with! From pops of colour to preppy style, greens add character to other colours, and they work as well in summer (lime greens) as they do in winter (khakis).

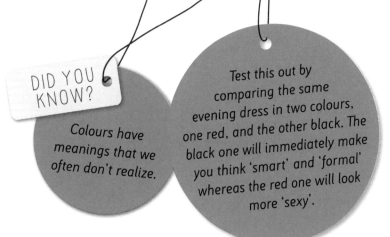

BLUES

Elegant or flashy, blues form a very broad palette. With blue, everything is possible!

PURPLES

Purples swing between warm and cool on the colour palette, depending on whether they contain more red or more blue – pair them accordingly.

PINKS

From juicy raspberry and baroque pink to romantic powder rose, the pink palette has vast potential. Choose a shade to fit with the style of your collection.

REDS

When it's bright scarlet, red is super dynamic. As it gets darker and more wine-coloured, it becomes more classic. Use in moderation.

GOLDS and SILVERS

Rarely used in clothes, these shades are particularly well suited to accessories. Golds are warm and add a touch of bling, while silvers are cool and elegant.

DESCRIBING YOUR COLOURS

There are hundreds of words for blending and distinguishing colours.
If you know the most common ones, you'll be able to explain your
choices more easily – and it's always better to
use the right terminology.

CONTRASTS
Combinations of colours that are opposite one another on the colour wheel (e.g. blue and orange), see page 18.

GRADATION
A single colour in all its shades, from the darkest through to the lightest.

MONOCHROME
Describes a colour scheme made up of various shades of a single colour.

HARMONY
The effect created by colours that go well together.

DEEP
Darker colours.

PASTEL
Light colours, created by adding white.

HUE
The pure form of a colour, without the addition of white or black.

SHADE
Darker and lighter variations of the same colour, created by adding more or less grey.

TOP TIP
The seasons will influence your choice of colours. People are more attracted to pastel colours in summer and to deeper colours in winter. Bear this in mind when making your selection.

ANDRÉ COURRÈGES

André Courrèges was born in Pau, France on 9th March 1923. He first became famous for his little white dress and colourful ankle boots, but now he's best known for using very bright colours in his designs.

His clothes used either plain, block colours like orange, green, purple, turquoise and yellow, or two-tone shades, and liberated the women of the 1960s and 70s thanks to their easy-to-wear, simple-looking shapes (though in fact they were technically very complex).

Still around today, his little vinyl jackets, stamped with a big 'AC', are a big hit with vintage fashion fans.

Create four colour schemes, representing each of
THE FOUR SEASONS.

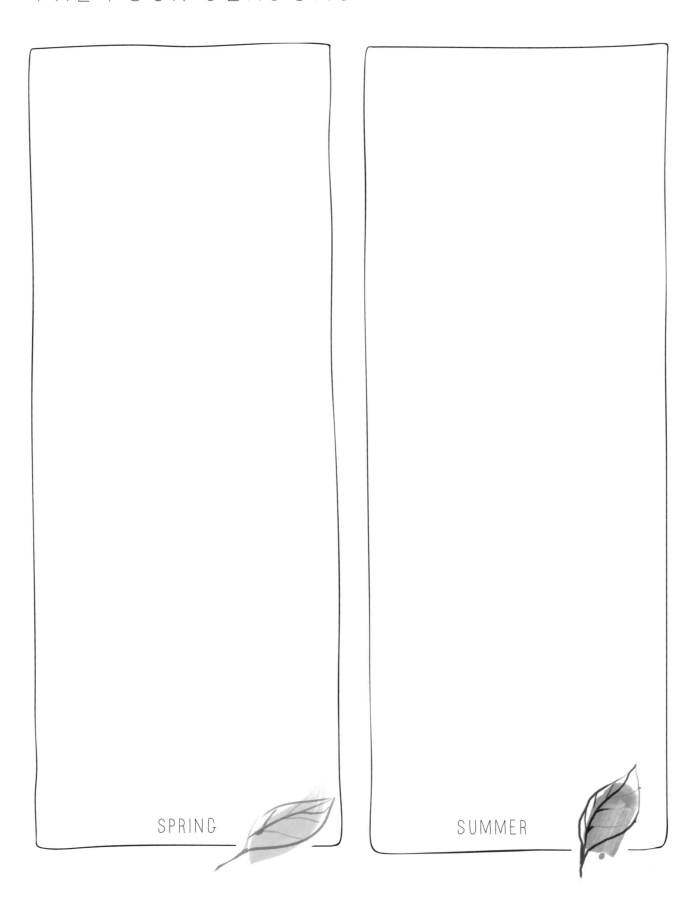

SPRING

SUMMER

TOP TIP

Get hold of some plastic wallets and use them to keep pages from magazines that show the biggest colour trends of the season. Put the pages in the wallets back-to-back, then store them in a file either in colour groups or by season and look through them regularly for inspiration.

AUTUMN

WINTER

CHOOSING THE RIGHT FABRICS

Choosing the right fabrics for your collection is even more important than picking the colour. This is what will decide whether your clothes hang properly or whether your dress is going to look like a sack.
It's your choice entirely, but don't forget that even if you find a fabric like wool itchy, you don't have to totally exclude it.

Read on for some advice on how to avoid giving your fans heatstroke in spring/summer, or freezing their fingers off in autumn/winter.

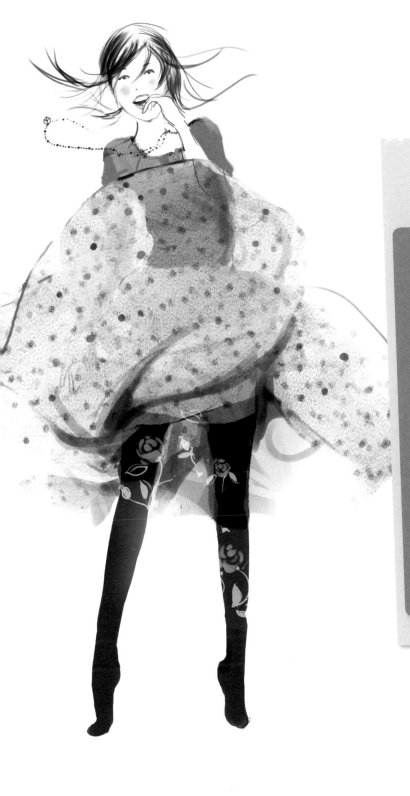

TOP TiP

Go into your own wardrobe, and select the clothes you feel comfortable in, and also those you don't. Have a look at what they are made of and work out which materials are the best for you.

You will see, for example, that cotton is comfortable but not very flowing, that linen is lovely to wear but creases very easily, and that synthetic fibres hang well but don't always feel that nice against your skin. When you do make your selection, remember that to improve the harmony of your collection it's best not to use too many different fabrics.

DID YOU KNOW?

There are two techniques for turning fibres into fabric: weaving and knitting. A third category that is known as 'non-woven' fabrics includes things like felt, lace and tulle.

Weaving

To weave a fabric, long threads (made of natural or synthetic fibres) are stretched vertically on a machine called a loom, and other threads are then interlaced between them horizontally. The vertical threads make up the **warp**, the horizontal threads are called the **weft**. The more threads that are added, in either direction, the heavier and more dense the material will be.

Once these fabrics are ready, you can use them just as they are, or print patterns on them to create what are called 'prints'.

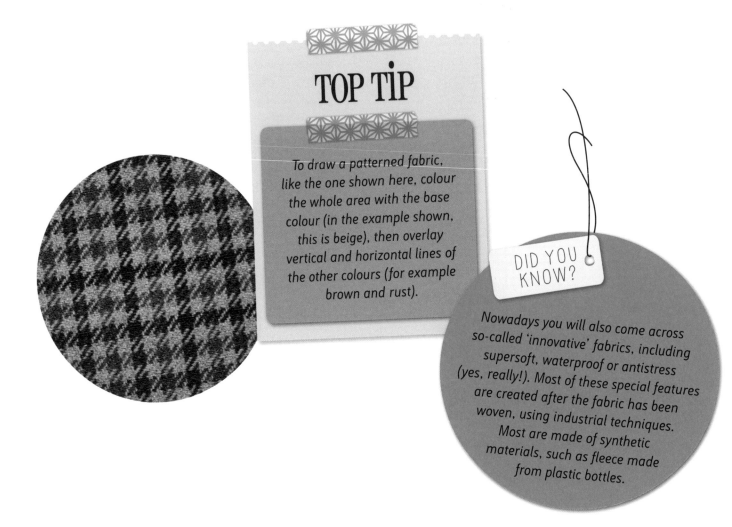

TOP TIP

To draw a patterned fabric, like the one shown here, colour the whole area with the base colour (in the example shown, this is beige), then overlay vertical and horizontal lines of the other colours (for example brown and rust).

DID YOU KNOW?

Nowadays you will also come across so-called 'innovative' fabrics, including supersoft, waterproof or antistress (yes, really!). Most of these special features are created after the fabric has been woven, using industrial techniques. Most are made of synthetic materials, such as fleece made from plastic bottles.

ÉMILIO PUCCI

Italy is one of the biggest producers of high-fashion clothing. This is down to the quality of its fabrics, but also to a designer called Emilio Pucci (1914 – 1992), whose prints were popular all over the world and were worn by the biggest stars of the 1950s and 60s. Marilyn Monroe in particular was a huge fan.

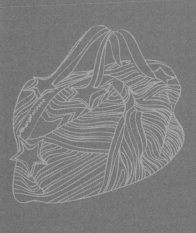

Pucci's designs are instantly recognizable, often incorporating multicoloured geometric patterns. The Pucci brand was revived in the 2000s by the founder's daughter Laudomia, and continues to dress today's celebrities, including Halle Berry and Kylie Minogue, as well as some mini stars such as Suri Cruise.

DRAW TWO DIFFERENT DESIGNS FOR PATTERNED PRINTS.

Get inspired by existing fabrics and put your own spin on them by changing the styles, the colours, or both.

To sketch a wool jumper, draw the contours on with slightly shaky lines. To show that you want a jacket to have a herringbone weave, there is no need to spend hours drawing the pattern all over the model. Draw it on just a small section of the front and the sleeve, and indicate what type of fabric should be used in a key at the side of your drawing.

DID YOU KNOW?

To make satin, the warp threads are longer than the weft.

To make velvet, another thread is added, which is pulled through to form a loop on the top surface of the fabric. You can either leave this as a loop, forming towelling, or you can cut it and create velvet.

KNITTING

Forget the big, itchy, ugly jumpers your grandmother knitted you that you then had to wear when you went to visit! Modern knitting machines use the same basic techniques as hand knitting, but they can knit every stitch you can imagine, from a simple jersey through to the most complex cable knit.

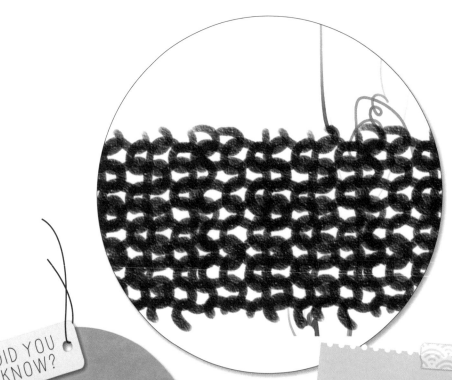

DID YOU KNOW?

A specialist can now create a jumper in only 45 minutes, including the finishing touches.

You waste much less material making knitted jumpers than clothes made with fabric, from which there are always edges and offcuts.

TOP TIP

There are dozens of different stitches in knitting. The finer they are, the more classic the jumper looks.

To give a more 'bohemian' look to your collection, include a jumper and cardigan made from a really chunky knit, either in natural wool, or with bright colours or a pattern.

SONIA RYKIEL

You can't miss her flamboyant hair ... but Sonia Rykiel is much more than an elegant redhead. Born on 25th May 1930, in Paris, France, she is in fact one of the most talented designers French fashion has ever known.

She rose to fame in 1962 when she designed a little grey fitted jumper. To her surprise, this piece of knitwear turned the fashion world upside down, and Sonia became well-known for using jersey and shorn velvet in her designs. Although her daughter now looks after the day-to-day running of the company, Sonia is still at the head of her large design empire, which ranges from fashion for men, women and children to interior design.

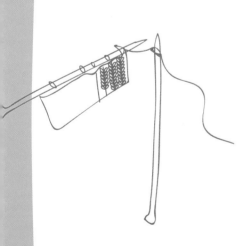

SeaSONaL COLLeCTIONS

Twice a year, designers rack their brains to come up with their next designs. It's a thrilling but tiring task. Thankfully, they have dozens of people in their teams who they can count on to help them out.

You might not have a large team to support you, but don't let that stop you from designing your first collection, just for you – one that shows off your personality.

TOP TIP

Every collection is a story. Start off by deciding on a theme – ideas will come more easily once that is fixed and you won't go off on a tangent.

Be like the professionals. Make a display board and stick everything on it that inspires you for your collection. Think outside the box. For example, if you have chosen a dramatic, gothic look, collect cuttings of architecture (churches, buildings), photos of paintings, postcards, portraits of famous people (present or past), paper or fabric in colours associated with those environments and glue or pin it all on to your board. This way, your sources of inspiration will always be in your sights.

For your next collection, take everything off the board and start again from scratch with the new theme you've chosen.

THE FASHION CALENDAR

To give you an idea of what your future diary could look like, here are the main phases in a designer's year.

JANUARY	FEBRUARY	MARCH	APRIL	MAY	JUNE
FINISH PRODUCTION OF THE SPRING/ SUMMER COLLECTION, PRIOR TO ITS DISTRIBUTION. MAKE THE PROTOTYPES FOR THE AUTUMN/WINTER COLLECTION.	REFINE THE AUTUMN/WINTER DESIGNS. CHOOSE MATERIALS FOR NEXT YEAR'S SPRING/SUMMER COLLECTION.	ASSESS WHICH OF THE CURRENT PIECES HAVE SOLD WELL, AND WHICH HAVE BEEN A COMPLETE FLOP IN THE SHOPS.	DRAW UP THE DESIGNS FOR NEXT YEAR'S SPRING/SUMMER LINE ...	PRODUCE THE AUTUMN/ WINTER COLLECTION.	

JULY	AUGUST	SEPTEMBER	OCTOBER	NOVEMBER	DECEMBER
CONTINUE PRODUCTION OF THE AUTUMN/WINTER RANGE.	FINISH PRODUCTION OF THE AUTUMN/WINTER COLLECTION.	DISTRIBUTE THE AUTUMN/WINTER COLLECTION.	FINISH DELIVERY OF THE AUTUMN/WINTER COLLECTION.	CONTINUE PRODUCTION FOR THE SPRING/SUMMER COLLECTION.	MAKE THE PROTOTYPES FOR THE AUTUMN/WINTER COLLECTION.
MAKE THE PROTOTYPES FOR THE SPRING/SUMMER COLLECTION.		REFINE THE DESIGNS FOR SPRING/SUMMER.

CHOOSE FABRICS FOR THE FOLLOWING YEAR'S AUTUMN/WINTER RANGE. | BEGIN PRODUCTION FOR THE SPRING/SUMMER RANGE.

ANALYZE SALES RESULTS. | DRAW DESIGNS FOR NEXT AUTUMN/WINTER. | START PRODUCTION OF SPRING/SUMMER COLLECTION. |

TOP TIP

It's time you chose your brand name! A first name, some initials, a word you like, anything goes. Don't forget to design your logo, too, either by hand or using fonts that you can find online.

Next, test your ideas out on your friends and make a final decision.

SPrING/SUMMEr

It's time to create your first collection! Start with spring/summer, the most vibrant, upbeat collection of the year.

But remember – just because the clothes are 'lighter' doesn't mean they'll be simpler to make, and even though the sun may be shining, it doesn't mean you should always choose fluorescent colours and a look that says 'just back from the beach'.

This is the moment to discover your own style and ask yourself some important questions. You'll find you discover a lot about your true tastes.

QUESTIONS

1. *Who are your favourite designers, and why?*

2. *Which shapes do you like wearing most in summer?*

3. *Do you love black, even in summer?*

4. *What sort of patterns do you like the best?*

5. *Who are you designing your collection for?*

TOP TiP

Clothes for women aren't the same as clothes for young girls. Always keep in mind what you would (or wouldn't) wear, choose your goal and stick to it.

Don't try to make designs that will please everyone, or you'll be sure to hit real problems.

ANSWERS

Here we go, you have chosen photos from magazines, you've gathered fabric samples you like and you're getting better and better at matching colours! It's time to make a selection from all those shades, to create a colour chart for your first collection.

COLOUR IN THIS CHART,
or stick cuttings on it to set the tones for your future designs.

TOP TIP

Think har-mo-ny! Focus on colours that not only go well with each other, but also blend with a wider range of colours. Spare a thought for your poor customers who will be standing in the shop wondering 'what on earth will I wear it with?'

Don't be afraid to be a little bit bold and daring, though – it's your collection after all.

CHOOSING YOUR FABRICS

This is a vital step in the development of your collection. To choose the fabric that best suits the look you're going for, you need to ask yourself some key questions:

• **Does the fabric match the season?**
Even if very lightweight cashmere can be worn in summer, it's better to avoid all wool fabrics unless you want to create a 'sauna' effect.

• **How does the fabric respond to heat?**
Synthetics tend to make people sweat more, so consider linen and cotton instead, which are light, floaty fabrics.

• **What are the current trends?**
Are stripes the latest popular thing? Slip a few into your collection!

• **Do you love a certain type of pattern?**
Use it as a base and make sure all your other fabrics are similar colours so you can keep your collection nicely co-ordinated.

• **Who are your clothes intended for?**
This will affect your fabric choices. For instance, chiffon may be perfect for gliding up the red carpet at a film premiere, but it's totally impractical for everyday teenage life.

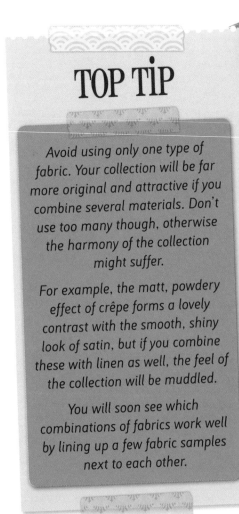

TOP TIP

Avoid using only one type of fabric. Your collection will be far more original and attractive if you combine several materials. Don't use too many though, otherwise the harmony of the collection might suffer.

For example, the matt, powdery effect of crêpe forms a lovely contrast with the smooth, shiny look of satin, but if you combine these with linen as well, the feel of the collection will be muddled.

You will soon see which combinations of fabrics work well by lining up a few fabric samples next to each other.

DRAW FABRICS AND PATTERNS ON THESE OUTFITS to fit the themes below:

A DAY TRIP
TO PARIS

A HOLIDAY
IN MIAMI

A STROLL IN
NEW YORK

A WEEKEND
IN ROME

TOP TiPS

Don't fall into the trap of making your outfits too obvious – for example choosing a beret and stripes for a day trip to Paris. Before you pick up your pencils, have a look at what popular designers in Europe and the USA are doing and take your inspiration from those trends.

As you start to draw your own designs, it's time to choose the technique that you're happiest with.

Pencils are good for drawing outlines, but too discreet to be able to distinguish shades of colours clearly. Felt tip is much better for that.

If you know how to work with watercolours or inks, you'll be able to give your drawings a softer and lighter feel.

CHOOSING YOUR STYLES

Now that you've chosen who your collection is for, you need to decide on the shapes of your clothes so they'll suit the people who are going to wear them.

To please as many people as possible, stick to simple shapes, flowing styles and relatively classic cuts. Don't forget that every item in your collection needs to go well with the others, so that your future customers will want to keep coming back for more of your clothes.

DRAW YOUR OWN TYPICAL STYLE on to this silhouette.

TOP TIP

If you're stuck on where to start, use your own personal clothing style as a springboard for your collection.

Little by little you can alter your look by changing the colours, shapes and styles until your collection becomes completely personal to you, and full of brand new ideas.

You might feel like standing out from the crowd straight away with super-innovative designs and elaborate shapes, but think carefully. Even Picasso learned how to draw people incredibly realistically before he created his stylized paintings.

So first of all, try to draw simple shapes and to understand how clothes are put together – that's the best way to get into the techniques.

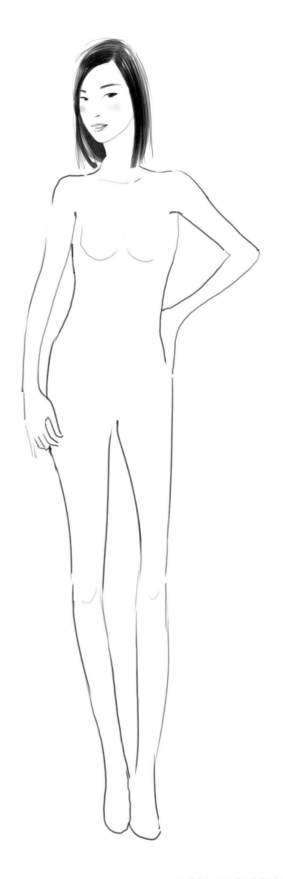

TYPES OF CLOTHING

DRESSES and SKIRTS

Women have traditionally worn dresses and skirts. They tended to be long and flowing, until in 1964, British stylist Mary Quant revolutionized fashion by launching the miniskirt. Young girls saw it as a way of gaining independence, and so it took off like wildfire.

Since then, nothing has been forbidden in fashion!

VIVIENNE WESTWOOD

Dame Vivienne Westwood is one of the UK's most recognizable fashion designers. With her flame-red hair and dramatic make-up, she's never afraid to stand out from the crowd. This bold and vibrant attitude is reflected in many of her designs.

Ever since she burst on to the scene with her first collection called 'Pirates' in 1981, she has fought against conformity and relished bringing something new, and sometimes shocking, to the catwalk. She is perhaps most famous for bringing 'punk' fashion – with its leather and rips, chains, spikes and safety pins – to the attention of a wider audience.

There are seven main dress shapes.
LEARN TO RECOGNIZE THEM and to draw
them yourself. You will be able to vary them in
endless ways to create your own designs.

BUBBLE

EMPIRE

BELTED

LOW-WAIST

TOP TiPS

Think about the movement you want your clothes to have. Use pleating to add structure, or alternatively focus on flowing, wide-skirted shapes, or fitted shift dresses.

To help you understand how a dress is cut, practise drawing out your own! For example, take one of your dresses and lay it out flat. Draw a vertical line down the middle of your page and draw one half of the dress, then the other. Outline the overall shape of the dress, then carefully draw the collar, sleeves, darts, buttons and even the seams. That will help you to see how it has been constructed, too.

FISHTAIL

A-LINE

SHIFT

HAVE FUN COLOURING THEM IN!

DRESS EACH MODEL IN A DIFFERENT TYPE OF DRESS, to match the styles below.

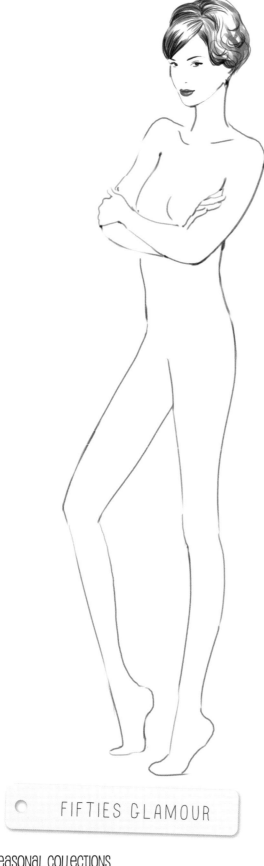

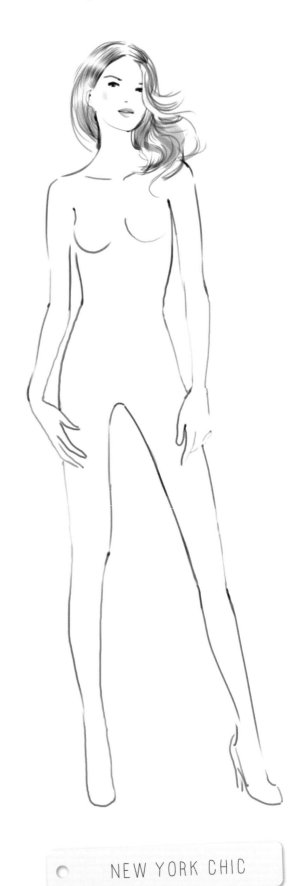

FIFTIES GLAMOUR

NEW YORK CHIC

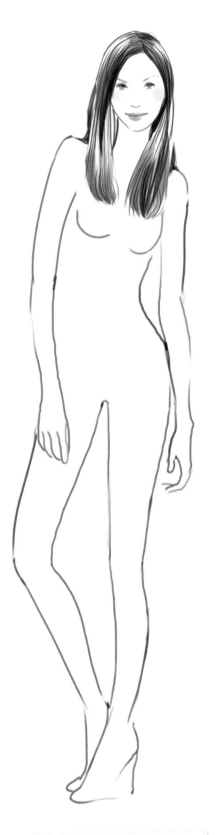

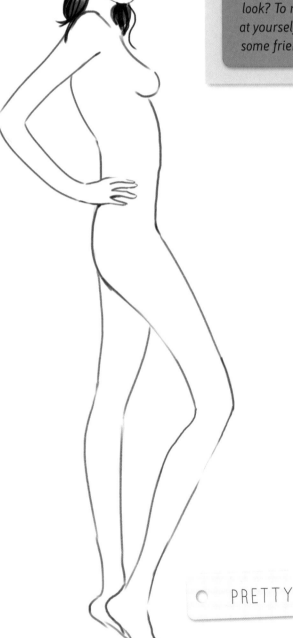

TOP TIP

While you're drawing, try to imagine how the fabric will hang. Which parts of the body will be in contact with the dress? How will the pleats look? To make it easier, look at yourself in a mirror, or ask some friends to pose for you.

PRETTY AND PREPPY

BOHO BEAUTY

TYPES OF CLOTHING

TROUSERS

Today they're a must-have in the world of women's fashion, but up until the 1960s, when designer André Courrèges made trousers more popular for women, skirts were still the norm. Wearing trousers was seen as daring and modern.

In 1965, the fashion industry produced more women's trousers than skirts for the first time in its history. A year later, Yves Saint Laurent dressed his models in suits, and since then, trousers have become both practical and stylish, and are found in every variation imaginable.

DID YOU KNOW?

Americans Jacob Davis and Levi Strauss had no idea they would be creating a legend when they decided to use a blue material made in Nîmes, France, known as denim (meaning 'from Nîmes'). Their aim at the time (1853), was just to produce very durable work trousers.

Mission accomplished! Jeans not only proved extremely hardwearing, but have also remained in fashion. Almost 2.3 billion pairs are sold every year, that's 73 every second.

YVES SAINT LAURENT

Yves Saint Laurent was only 21 years old when he launched his first collection, at Dior, in 1958. Four years later, he was already flying free and bringing his own style to the whole world, reinventing the safari jacket, the pea coat, the trouser suit and the tuxedo for women.

Born in Oran, Algeria, on 1st August 1936, he remained at the head of his multinational company alongside his long-term business partner Pierre Bergé, until a few months before his death in 2008.

Trousers come in lots of different shapes.
LEARN HOW TO RECOGNIZE AND
DRAW SOME OF THE MAIN ONES.

SKINNY

PEG LEG

STRAIGHT LEG

COMBAT

HAVE FUN COLOURING THEM IN!

To avoid a 'shapeless' look, pair wide trousers with a figure-hugging top. Try to match wider tops with a slimmer legged trouser. And combine your straight-leg trousers with a blouse for guaranteed style.

DID YOU KNOW?

Although tracksuit trousers can be very fashionable and even cost as much as a pair of designer jeans, if you want to keep them looking up-market you will need to make them from materials like velvet, crêpe or satin, and in sensible, neutral colours.

JODHPUR

FLARE

BOYFRIEND

DRESS EACH OF THESE MODELS IN THE SAME TROUSER STYLE (choose one from page 58-59), but pair it with different tops so as to create four distinct styles.

Give a name to each of
the styles you've created.

TOP TIP

*Don't forget the pockets! Collect photos or sketch out
all the types of pocket that you can find.
There are dozens of different shapes.
Practise drawing them and then adding them
to your clothing designs.*

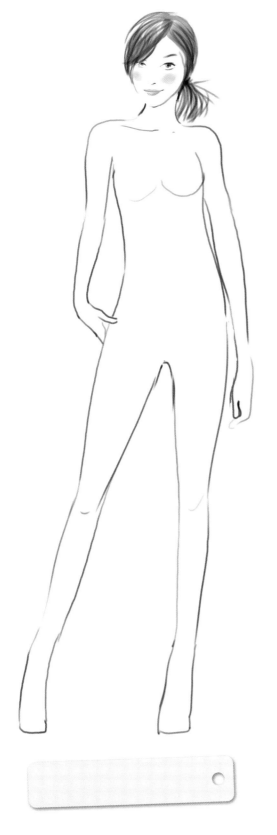

AUTUMN/ WINTER

Professionals have to design their autumn/winter styles a whole year before they go on sale.

With your Fashion Book, you're free to draw your own autumn/ winter collection whenever you feel like it, even while drinking lemonade in the sunshine. Make sure you always have the season in mind though. Be careful not to make your coats as thin as tissue paper or too tight-fitting, or how will you get them on over your favourite big, cosy winter jumper?

CHOOSING YOUR COLOURS AND FABRICS

Except for the coats in your collection, which need to be made out of strong, warm fabric, don't waste your time searching for special 'winter materials'. Wool, cashmere and flannel are bound to be cosy, but cotton and even crêpe will work, too, when paired with a thick jacket. Try to avoid fleece though, because warm though it may be, it's really only for country walks and it's tough to make it look stylish.

TOP TIP

If you don't have a fabric shop nearby, browse online instead. There are dozens of sites offering all the different fabric types available. It's sure to give you tons of inspiration.

Burberry

Thomas Burberry (1835 – 1926) invented a way of weaving fabric that would change the world of fashion. Burberry created 'gabardine', a water resistant material, and the fashion icon that is the Burberry trench coat was born.

Initially, trench coats were about function over fashion – they were worn by soldiers heading off to war. Over the years, the trench has evolved to become an absolute staple in the fashion world.

In 1920, the now famous Burberry check was used as a lining for the trench coats. This tartan pattern was one of Burberry's most distinctive hallmarks in the 20th century, and cemented Burberry's position as one of the top UK fashion houses.

MAKE FOUR COLOUR CARDS showing the colour schemes you've chosen for your autumn/winter collection.

TOP TIP

To give your collection more character and 'oomph', include the same pattern on several items. Sometimes use it all over, and sometimes just use a touch here and there – for example, a blouse and a jacket trimmed with the same fabric.

CHOOSING YOUR STYLES

Fashion evolves in cycles. You might think the clothes you wore ten years ago
are terribly dated, but they could be a huge trend ... in ten years time!
To help you, here is a list of some styles that simply never date,
and a handful that keep on coming back into fashion.

TIMELESS STYLE

Blazers, trench coats, military
(or army) jackets, straight-leg
trousers, jeans, plain T-shirts, twin
sets (matching top and cardigan),
black, beige, navy blue, white.

OFTEN IN FASHION

Certain trouser styles (slim, baggy,
pleated waist, turn-ups), shoulder
pads, duffle coats, shorts and cropped
trousers, very slim waists (or no waist
at all), stripes, flowery fabrics, lace,
berets, asymmetrical cuts, bright
or fluorescent colours, such as pink,
yellow or turquoise.

TOP TIP

Try to put at least a couple of classic
styles that won't date into your
collection. That way, you'll be sure
to attract all sorts of customers, and
they might also fall in love with some
of your other items.

STICK IN PICTURES FROM MAGAZINES

showing clothes that you think will never go out of style.

DRESS THESE MODELS in some of the key pieces from your autumn/winter collection.

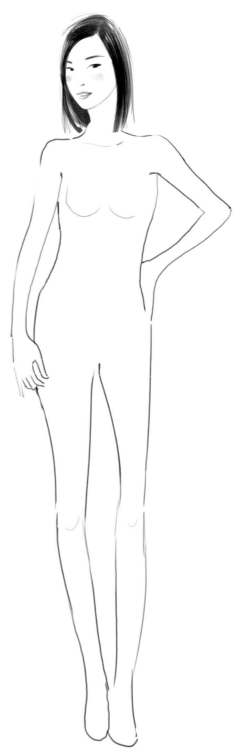

TOP TIP

Your clothes won't hang well if your silhouette isn't correctly proportioned. Use the 'head' measurement technique on page 10 to help you, make sure your outlines always have shoulders 1.5 heads wide, waists 1 head wide, and hips 1.5 heads across.

TYPES OF CLOTHING

COATS & JACKETS

The growth of unisex fashion has shaken up the world of coats. Parkas were previously only worn by men, but they're now the in-thing for fashionable girls. Even so, some people still prefer a good old coat, but remember that 'classic' doesn't always have to mean 'old fashioned'. It's up to you to study the latest trends and adapt your designs to fit the newest fashions. Once again, always keep in mind who your target is, and put yourself in your future buyers' shoes.

DID YOU KNOW?

Coats, parkas and other winter jackets are often made using expensive materials, and they can require a large quantity of fabric. To avoid breaking the bank, designers usually limit themselves to three or four of these garments in each collection.

TOP TIP

Think about how your jacket or coat will fasten. Look into different buttons, zips, toggles, poppers and loops. These are the details that will give your designs real personality.

Learn to draw them, using photos from magazines or websites as your starting point, then add them to your coat designs.

accessories

Whether you go for understated and elegant, or bright and bold with pops of colour, choosing the right accessories is a vital step in completing your collection.

Bags

There's no doubt that a handbag is an absolute essential to complete your look. Bags can make some fashionistas hysterical as soon as they arrive in the shops. While some girls remain loyal to a particular style or label, others prefer to collect a variety, so as to have a beautiful bag to match each outfit.

The designer's aim is to come up with <u>the</u> It bag that everyone will go crazy about. Some have succeeded, so why not have a go, too?

DRAW YOUR PERFECT BAG (inside and out). It could be the next 'It bag' for the next 'It girl'.

Jewellery

There are very few high street clothes shops that don't have a jewellery section. Whether they're near the till or draped on the models in the window, those beaded necklaces and sparkling earrings are simply crying out for you to take them home ... it's hard to resist.

This is one way for brands to boost their sales, with products that are usually cheap to produce. It's also a great way for those customers who aren't feeling inspired to be sure they have the 'right' accessory and won't risk a fashion fail.

DID YOU KNOW?

Some designers create their own jewellery range, but most work with specialist jewellery makers. Others buy from large companies called 'wholesalers' who give them ready-made pieces that match their collections.

TOP TiP

You'll find plenty of inspiration not only in fashion boutiques, but also in museums. Women have been wearing jewellery for thousands of years, so exhibitions and paintings can be a goldmine for new ideas. Always carry something to sketch on, so that you won't forget what you've seen.

ACCESSORIZE THESE MODELS AND MAKE THEM SUPER-STYLISH.

Add earrings, bangles, rings and necklaces.
Let your imagination run wild.

TOP TIP

Practise drawing faces with different expressions (have a look at some magazines for ideas), so that your model's look suits the style of your clothes and accessories as closely as possible. You'll know as soon as you hit on the right combination – everything will come together.

Hats

Any designer can dream up a good hat design, but to turn ideas into hats you'll need a professional hat maker, called a milliner. They will mould the felt or weave the straw to create the design you've come up with – whether it's classic or completely wild and wacky. Lots of milliners are designers in their own right, too.

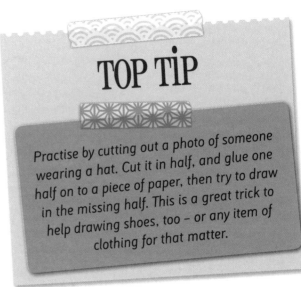

TOP TIP

Practise by cutting out a photo of someone wearing a hat. Cut it in half, and glue one half on to a piece of paper, then try to draw in the missing half. This is a great trick to help drawing shoes, too – or any item of clothing for that matter.

PHILIP Treacy

Born in Ireland in 1967, Philip Treacy is world famous for his sculptural hats, and many internationally recognized models, actresses and celebrities can often be seen sporting some of his fabulous headwear. 'A hat is a positive symbol,' he says. 'A good hat is the ultimate glamour accessory. It thrills observers and it makes the wearer feel a million dollars.'

While studying at the National College of Art and Design in London, Treacy made hats 'as a hobby' to go with the outfits he was designing as part of his course. His hats were spotted by legendary stylist Isabella Blow, and from then on it was clear that he'd found his true calling.

Treacy has designed for Chanel, Alexander McQueen, Valentino and Ralph Lauren, and in 2007 he was awarded an OBE for services to the British fashion industry.

SHOES

Shoemaking is a very technical profession. Some big brands create shoe collections alongside their clothing and accessory ranges, but others stick solely to shoes. These are crucial accessories for your future fashion show. Whether you go for flats or choose skyscraper heels, the models will strut their stuff in your choice.

TOP TIP

Your figures' feet can be entirely realistic and drawn exactly to scale, but your models will have a bit more character if you exaggerate the size and curve of their feet (slightly!).

CHRISTIAN LOUBOUTIN

Born in 1964 in Paris, France, Christian Louboutin started his career in shoe design alongside famous French shoemakers Charles Jourdan and Roger Vivier. In 1992 he chose to go his own way, and opened a boutique in Paris.

His very personal way of revisiting the classic styles attracts a celebrity clientele who snap up his designs, and Anna Wintour, the editor of Vogue who is famously difficult to impress, recently wrote two articles praising him.

His signature red-soled shoes are nowadays seen from Los Angeles to Paris, New York to Moscow and São Paulo, and regularly appear on the catwalk and on red carpets all over the world.

DID YOU KNOW?

Some top designers work with shoemakers who create special shoes for them, like Raymond Massaro for Chanel, for example. Make sure the shoes you choose fit the overall look of your collection.

Haute couture

In the fashion world, there is a special category, called 'haute couture', which is reserved for the crème de la crème of fashion design houses. These are the smallest, most artistic fashion houses that focus on tailor-made outfits, each unique or in a very limited edition, personally designed and made in the designer's own workshops from the best materials available.

In 1945, there were more than 100 haute couture fashion houses, but nowadays there are only a handful left, and most of these are in France. Haute couture clothes cost thousands of pounds to buy, because they are often unique.

TOP TIP

Even though clothes from haute couture houses are unaffordable, don't hesitate to poke your nose in through the door of their boutiques, or visit their floor of the department store. You'll often find dozens of ideas there for developing your own collections.

Leave all practicalities aside and go wild
DESIGNING AN HAUTE COUTURE PIECE.

TOP TIP

Think overstated luxury. You could dream up a princess ballgown encrusted with crystals, or something bright and floaty in exotic silks.
There are no limits ...

WOrTH

French haute couture was
invented by ... an Englishman!
Born in 1825, Charles Frederick
Worth arrived in Paris when he
was 20. In 1858, he founded his
fashion house with a Swedish
partner, Otto Bobergh.

By 1871 he was in charge of
a house that was dressing the
biggest names of the moment,
from empresses to the most
popular actresses of the times. His
recipe for success? To present a
new collection every year – and so
haute couture was born.

Haute Couture
&
Ready to Wear

Ready-to-wear clothing, sometimes also known as 'prêt-à-porter', is the opposite of haute couture. Ready-to-wear clothes are produced in large numbers and standard sizes, for people to buy without needing bespoke alterations. Ready-to-wear clothes have a huge market. Nowadays there are hundreds of ready-to-wear designers across the USA and in Europe. The clothes are designed in the Western world, but they are usually made in the East.

DID YOU KNOW?

Coco Chanel once said, 'fashion does not exist unless it goes down into the streets'. The brand that bears her name has been an important player in both haute couture and ready-to-wear collections for many years.

COCO CHANEL

'An extraordinary destiny' is the best way to describe the life of Gabrielle Bonheur Chanel, known as Coco Chanel. She was abandoned by her father at the age of 12 and sent, along with her two sisters, to an orphanage in Corrèze, France where she stayed for six years. At 18, she went to a convent, where she learnt dressmaking.

She opened her first hat shop in Paris in 1910. A few years later, she designed her first clothing and jewellery styles, which were a marvellous combination of city chic and understated elegance. The Second World War forced her to close, but she started her fashion house up again in 1954 and launched the look that made her name: suits with two-tone court shoes. She died on 10th January 1971, aged 87.

ON THE
CATWALK

Stress ... excitement ... adrenaline – the day of the fashion show is here! At last, your collection will be shown off in public. You've been planning it carefully, refining every detail for months so that it will all go smoothly.

Music, lights, choice of models, nothing must be left to chance, and given the tens of millions of pounds involved, that's just as well.

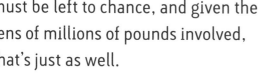

MODELS AND THE PODIUM

Up-and-coming models, international supermodels, 'It girls' ... they are all chosen for their figures and their personal style, which matches the look of the particular fashion house they're modelling for. Notice that if some models always look like they're sulking, it's usually because they've been asked to. Some are even so used to putting on this blank expression that the designers have to remind them before they go on, 'Don't forget to smile, girls!'

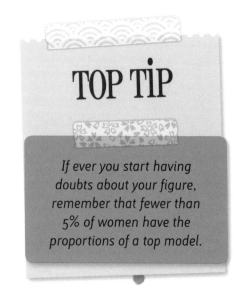

TOP TIP

If ever you start having doubts about your figure, remember that fewer than 5% of women have the proportions of a top model.

DID YOU KNOW?

Designers give names to each of their styles. Some name them according to the theme of the collection, others simply follow the alphabet: each item in collection 'A' has a name beginning with A, and so on. Not terribly original, but quite practical when it comes to locating them.

ALEXANDER MCQUEEN

Lee Alexander McQueen
(1970 – 2010) was known
worldwide for his flair for drama on
the catwalk. He created large-scale
theatrical fashion shows that left
audiences open-mouthed.

From 1999's spring/summer
collection, which saw a model in
a plain white dress being sprayed
by robotic paint guns at the end of
the catwalk, to a large glass box
containing a model surrounded by
fluttering moths in 2001 – every
show was a brilliant piece of
performance art. After his death in
2010, his assistant, Sarah Burton,
took over as head of the McQueen
fashion house.

HAIRSTYLISTS, MAKE-UP ARTISTS, DRESSERS ...

In fashion week, models perform at one fashion show after another, so they often arrive late ... and completely exhausted.

Don't panic! The hair and make-up magicians know how to pep up any tired-looking face. In their expert hands, the girls emerge looking fresh and ready to step straight into the character they've been asked to represent.

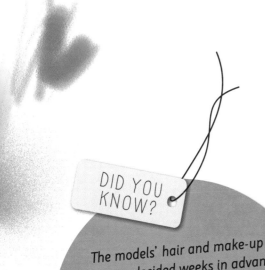

DID YOU KNOW?

The models' hair and make-up styles are decided weeks in advance, in consultation with the designer, according to the 'story' they want to tell on the catwalk. Once it has all been agreed, the top hair and make-up artists explain the exact style they have to create to the army of professionals who will be working at each show.

COPY THE HAIRSTYLE ON TO EACH OF THESE FACES. Then add make-up to give them their own personalities.

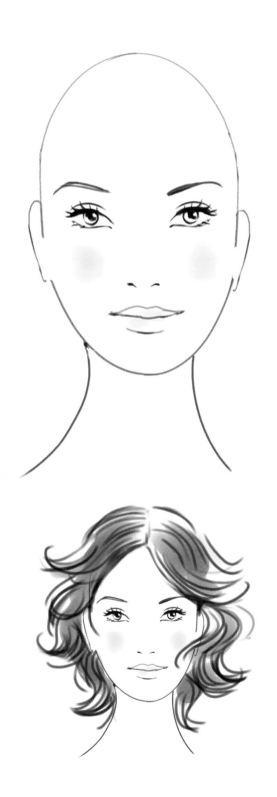

FINISHING TOUCHES

Now that you have finished designing your collection, it's time to create your brand's label. This will be the one that's attached to all the cool clothes you've designed.

TOP TIPS

If you have gone for a simple style, your label should reflect this. A black or navy blue label with the name of your brand written in white or gold would be a classy and elegant option.

If you prefer a quirkier, colourful style, why not match your label with one of the patterned fabrics you've included in your range? Make sure the brand name is still readable. White labels tend to go yellow and don't have much character, but if you write your brand name in a bold font, your label will definitely get noticed.

The choice of material often comes down to price: fabric or plastic can be very pretty or eye-catchingly original, but they are expensive! Printing labels on thin card remains a classic and affordable option.

To attach the label, raffia is perfect if you are using natural cardboard, a little gold thread goes best with a navy blue or black label and gold writing, while a red ribbon will add a vibrant touch to a white label.

Square, rectangular, round ... there are so many shape options. Choose the one that will go best with your brand style. For example, if your brand name is long, it's all very well wanting to cram it into a heart-shaped label but if no-one can read it it won't be much use!

Unless you really want to make a statement, labels aren't usually larger than eight or ten centimetres. Stay modest but don't go too tiny – your label still needs to be seen.

Go to the shops and look at what the brands there do. After all, they employ a whole army of marketing experts to answer all these questions for them. Take note of their ideas to help with yours.

Decide what colour, shape, size and material your label is going to be. Choose one of these examples to get you started, or DESIGN YOUR OWN.

IMAGINE A MAGAZINE ARTICLE about your collection. Write a little feature about the designer – that's you! Explain what inspired you, and why you made the choices you did.

Then scan in or copy a few of your clothing designs.
Try to put all of it together on this page so that it
looks like a real magazine article.

YOUR DESIGNER SKETCHBOOK

Practice! There's nothing like it for helping you improve your skills and discover your own style. The next pages in this book are yours to fill with your own designs, and kick-start your first collection.

As you get more confident with your drawings, you won't need the pre-drawn model outlines in this book to help you – you'll be ready to sketch your own designs on blank pages, from scratch. If you've followed all the top tips in these pages, you'll be well on your way to some freestyle fashion design.

Once you've filled the pages at the back of this book, treat yourself to a new sketchbook, big enough to give you room for drawing, but small enough to carry with you all the time. The paper should be nice and thick, so that your drawings don't show through from one page to the next. Personalize it with your own cuttings – photos of models, clothes by your favourite designers or maybe even the business card of a cute shop you've discovered. This sketchbook should reflect who you are and what you love most.

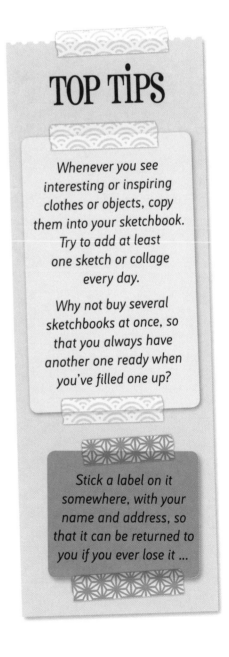

TOP TIPS

Whenever you see interesting or inspiring clothes or objects, copy them into your sketchbook. Try to add at least one sketch or collage every day.

Why not buy several sketchbooks at once, so that you always have another one ready when you've filled one up?

Stick a label on it somewhere, with your name and address, so that it can be returned to you if you ever lose it ...

COMPLETE THESE
MODELS with your
own fabulous designs.

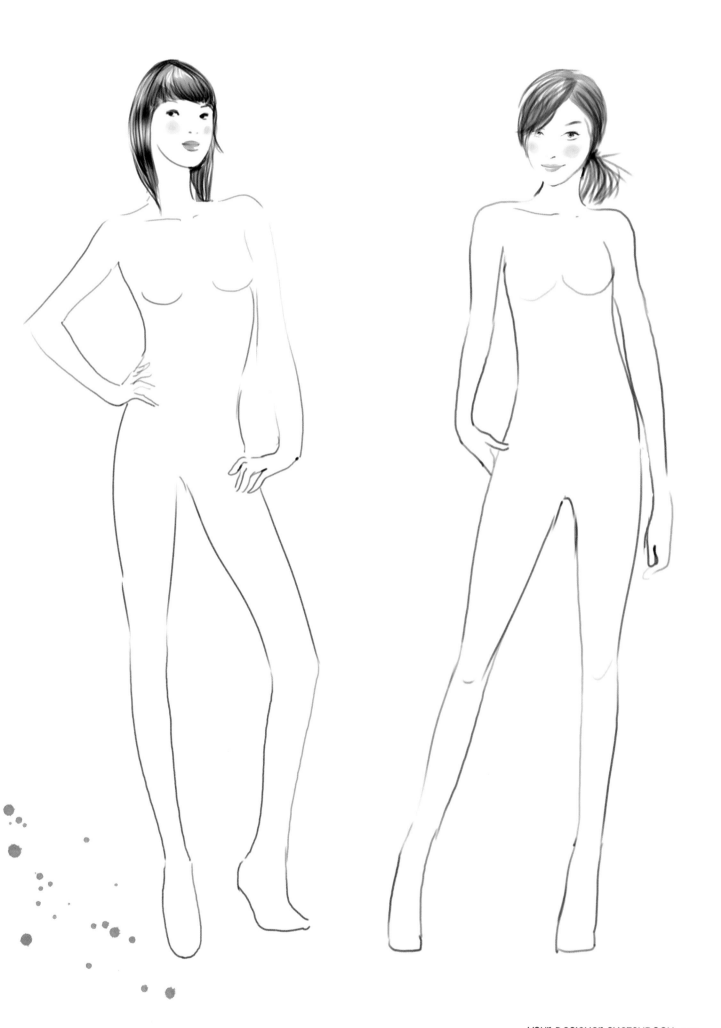

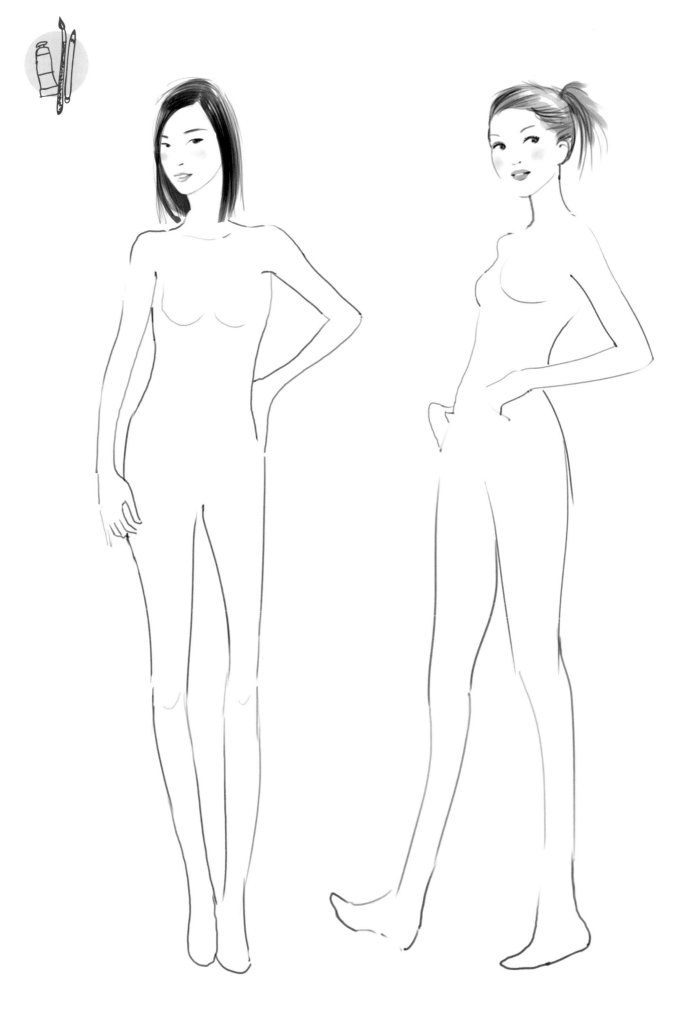

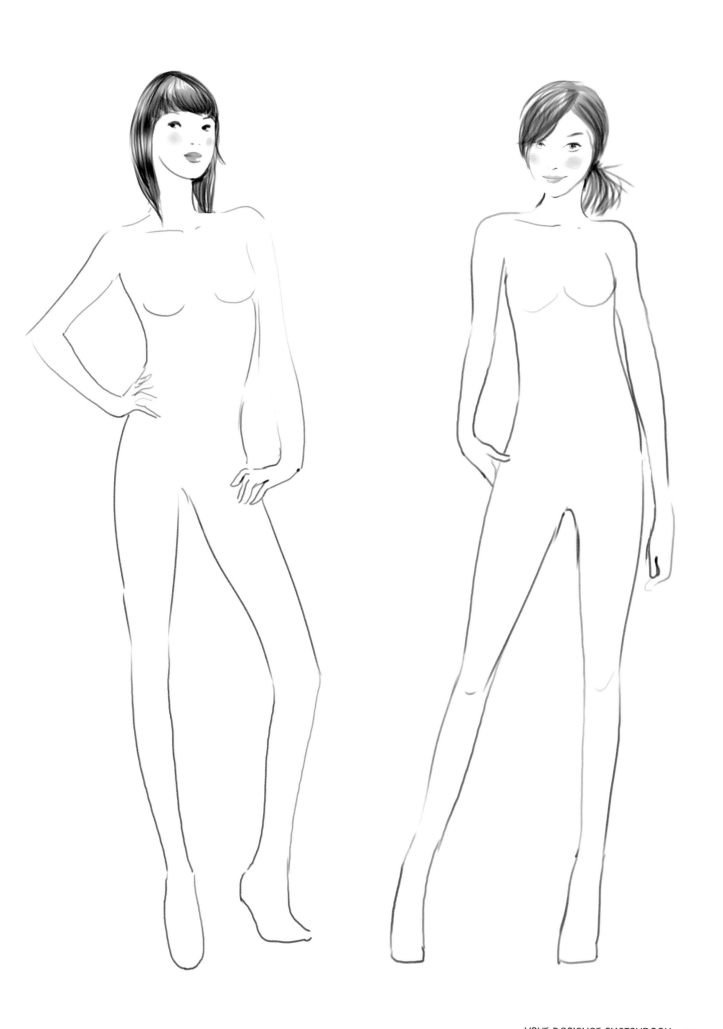

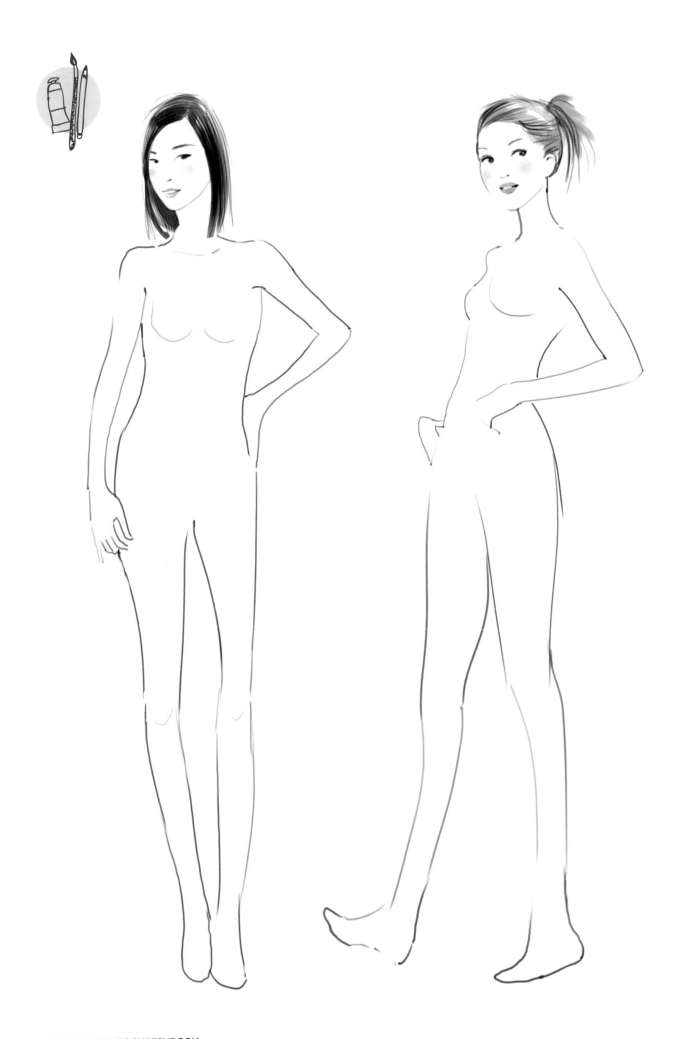

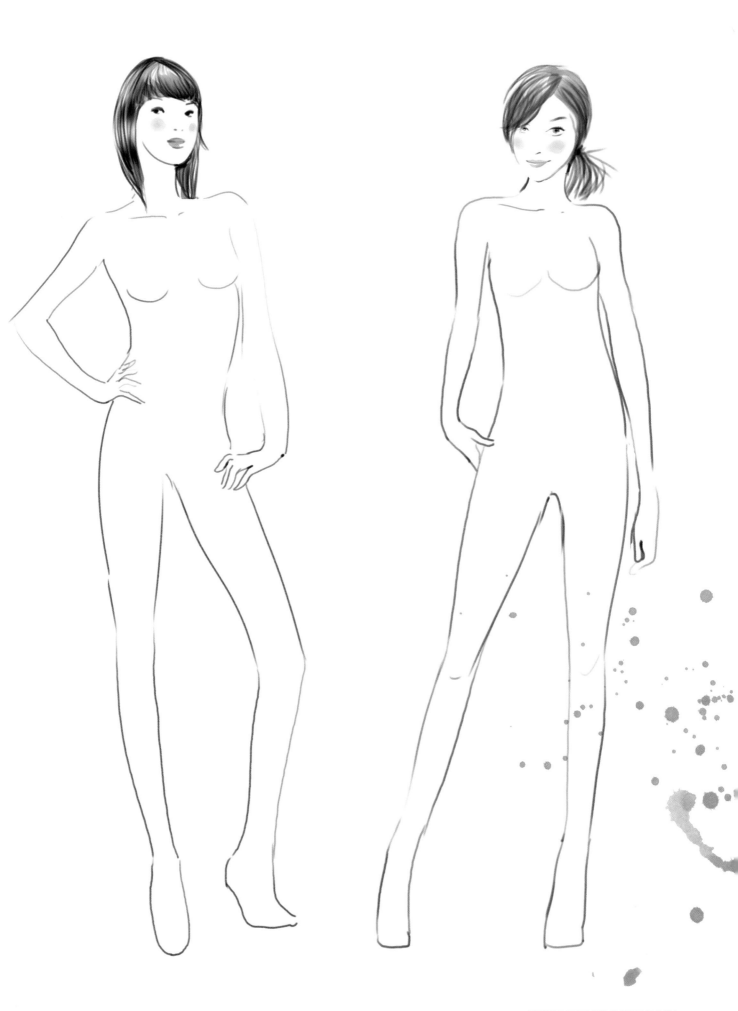

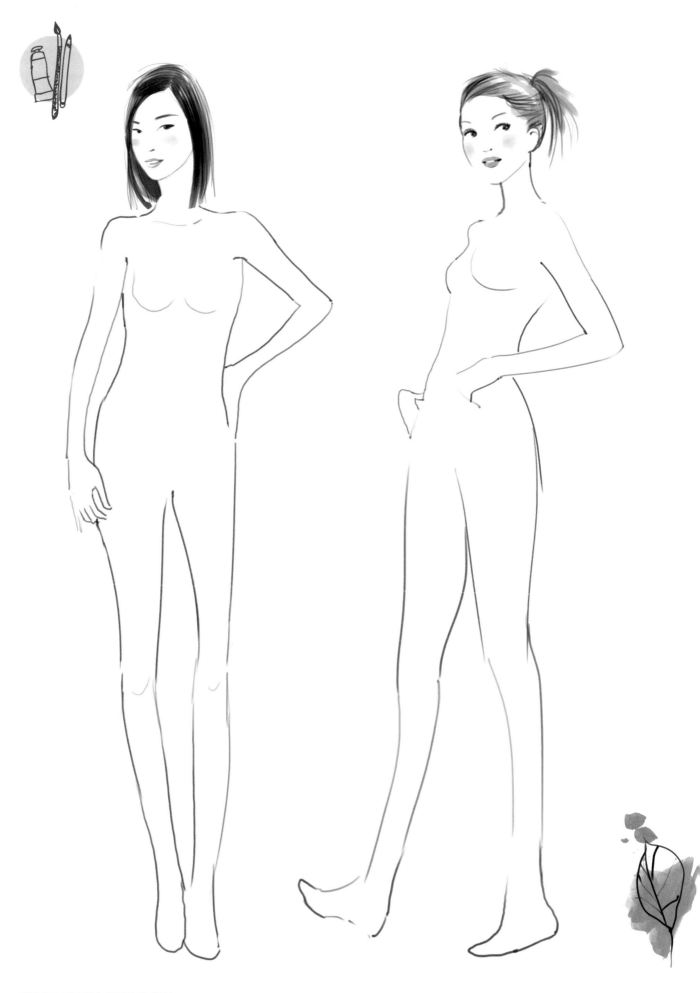

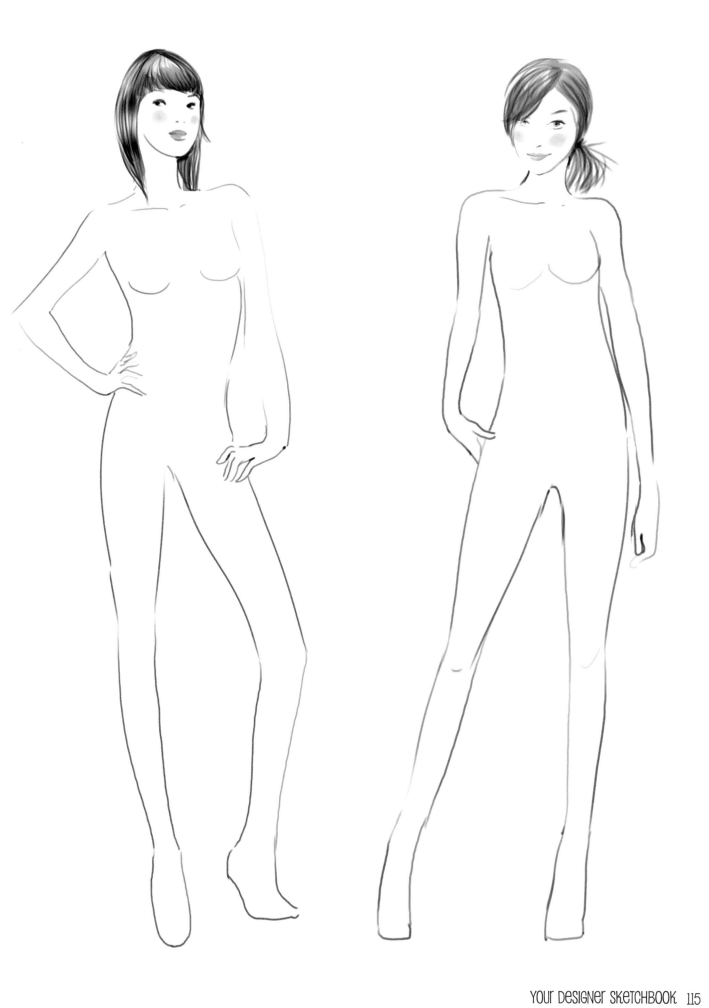

THESE BLANK PAGES ARE FOR YOU.
You can use them to draw your first models entirely from scratch.

TOP TIP

If you have real difficulty with faces, stylize them by simply indicating an oval for the head, and adding the hair.

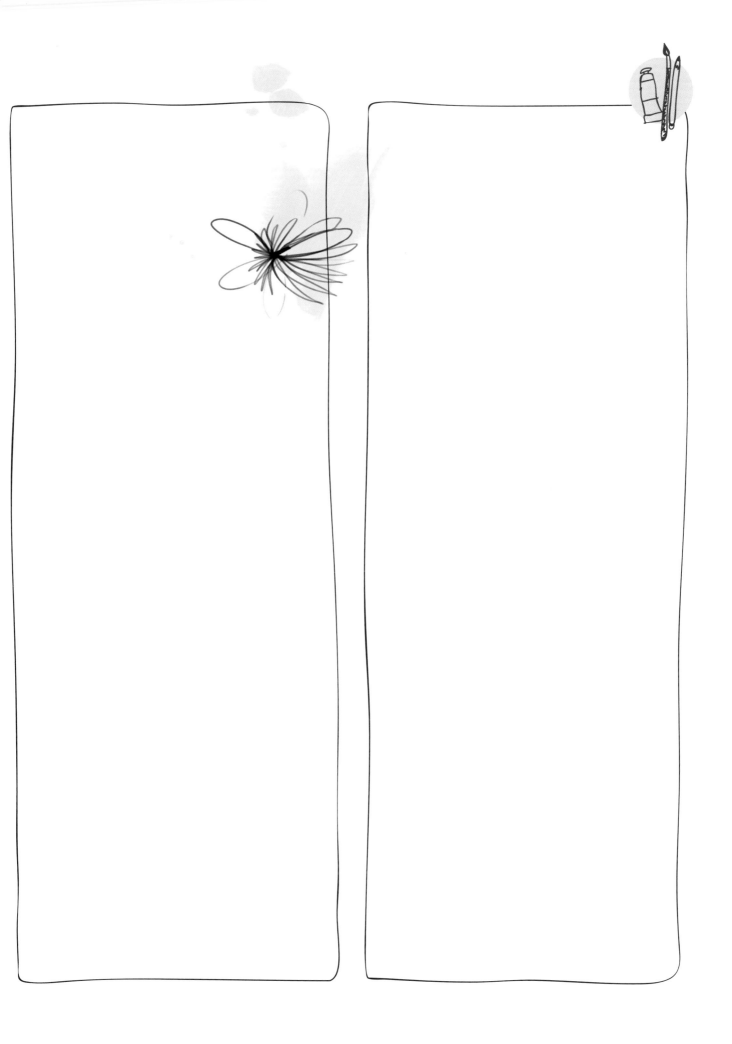

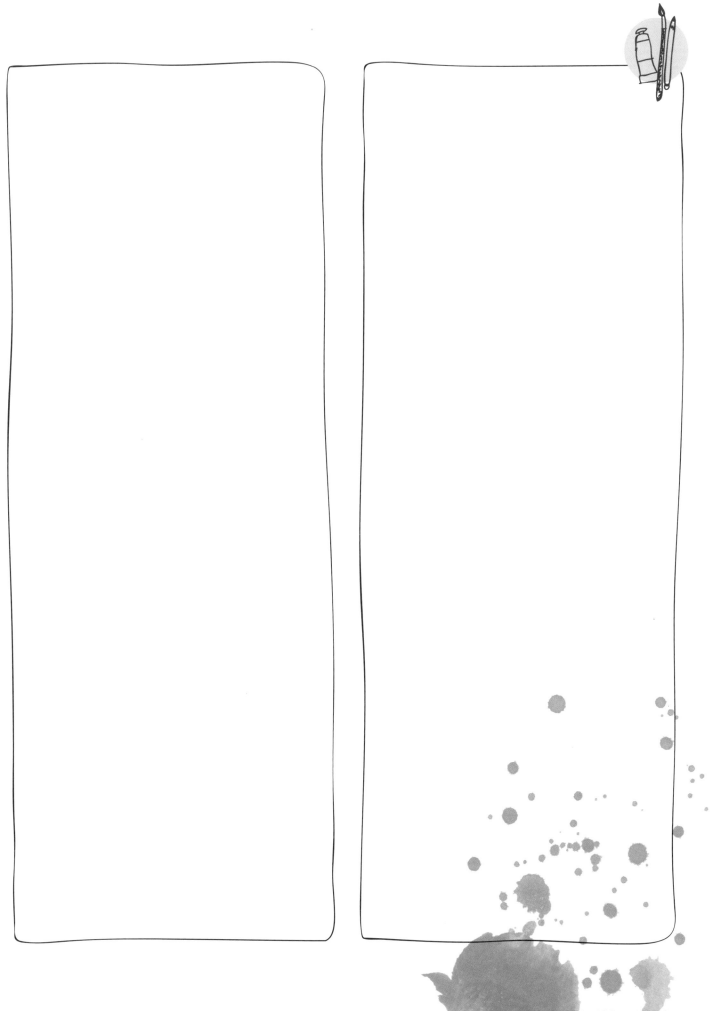

YOU WILL also LOVE ...

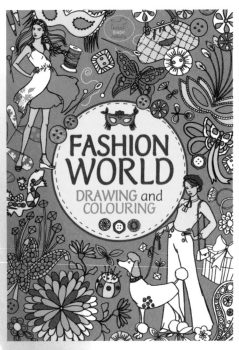

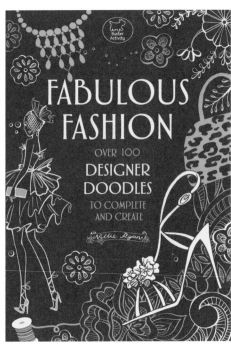

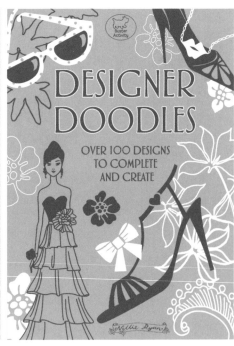

ISBN: 978-1-78055-011-4

ISBN: 978-1-907151-84-2

ISBN: 978-1-906082-61-1